Timothy Shay Arthur

The Lost Children

And Other Stories

Timothy Shay Arthur

The Lost Children
And Other Stories

ISBN/EAN: 9783337005030

Printed in Europe, USA, Canada, Australia, Japan

Cover: Foto ©Thomas Meinert / pixelio.de

More available books at **www.hansebooks.com**

INNOCENCE.

Page 37.

THE

LOST CHILDREN,

AND

OTHER STORIES.

By T. S. ARTHUR.

WITH ILLUSTRATIONS FROM ORIGINAL DESIGNS BY CROOME.

PHILADELPHIA:
J. B. LIPPINCOTT & CO.
1863.

CONTENTS.

	PAGE
THE LOST CHILDREN	7
HARSH WORDS AND KIND WORDS	14
THE DRUNKARD'S GOOD ANGELS	23
GOOD AND EVIL ANIMALS	37
THE MOTHER'S GRAVE	40
THE STORY OF THE LITTLE LAMB	50
THE YOUNG TEACHER	55
A CONVERSATION	69
SPEAK KINDLY	72
I CAN'T DO IT	85
A GENTLEMAN	92
THE SABBATH-SCHOOL	97
FIRST EARNINGS	103
GOD SEES US	129
THE PET SPARROW	133
THE POWER OF KIND WORDS	150

THE LOST CHILDREN.

THE LOST CHILDREN.

"TELL us the story about the lost children, dear mother," said George, laying down his playthings and coming to his mother's side.

"Oh, yes, do, mother, please," added the little boy's sister; a bright-eyed, rosy-cheeked girl, just ten years old.

"I told you the story yesterday," replied the mother.

"I know you did," answered George. "But we want to hear it again. Tell it to us, dear mother, and we will be such good children!"

"There was once a little boy and girl," began the mother; "no older than you are, my children, who got lost in a thick, dark wood, in which were fierce wild beasts. They were brother and sister, and their names were Edward and Ellen. They were playing near their father's house one day, when Edward said, 'Come, sister, let us go across the field into the woods yonder, and gather some pretty flowers for mamma.'

"Ellen was pleased at the thought of getting for her dear mamma a beautiful bunch of flowers, and so she said, 'Oh, yes, brother, let us go.'

"So this little boy and girl went across the field and into the woods, where they wandered about, gathering a great many bright wild flowers. When their hands were full, Ellen said, 'Now, brother, let us go home.'

"They took hold of each other's hands and started, as they thought, toward their home; but I am sorry to say they went away from, instead of toward their home, and soon found that they were lost in a thick, dark wood. Poor Ellen began to

THE LOST CHILDREN.

cry. Edward put his arm around her, and said—

"'Don't cry, sister, we will find our way home.'

"'Oh, no, Edward," she said, 'we are lost in the woods, and it will soon be dark. Oh! we shall be eaten up by the wolves.'

"' The wolves will not eat us up,' replied the brave-hearted little boy, confidently. 'So don't cry, sister.'

"'Oh, yes, I am sure they will.'

"'Don't be afraid. I know they won't hurt us. Wolves are wicked animals, but if we pray to God to take care of us, He will not let the wolves hurt us.'

"'Oh, let us pray then,' said Ellen. And all alone in the gloomy forest, this dear little boy and his sister knelt down and prayed that God would keep the wicked wolves from hurting them.'

"After they had prayed, Ellen's tears dried up, and she took hold of Edward's arm, and clung close to his side. Just then a deep growl sounded through the forest, and presently they saw a long gray wolf coming fiercely toward them.

"The children dropped upon their knees, and Edward said aloud—

"'Our Father in heaven, keep the wolves from hurting us.'

"They had no sooner prayed that prayer than the wolf stopped right still for a minute or two, and then ran off another way.

"They were very much frightened, and trembled all over. Ellen said—

"'God has made the wicked wolf go away—He will not let him hurt us. Oh, I wish He would show us the way home. It is getting so dark.'

"'Let us ask Him to show us the way home,' said Edward.

"Again the lost children knelt down and prayed. They were still on their knees when they heard afar off, the sound of their father's voice calling them. Oh! how their little hearts jumped for joy. They sprang up, and ran as fast as they could in the direction from which the sound came. In a little while they were in their father's arms, crying for joy."

"I am so glad!" exclaimed George and his sister at once; "God wouldn't let the wicked wolf eat them up."

"No, my children. He kept them from all harm. And if you will be good, and pray to him, He will protect you in every danger."

"Don't you know any more stories about lost children, dear mother?" asked George.

"Shall I tell you about the Children of Men, who were once lost in the Wilderness of Sin?"

"Oh, yes, do mother. But who were the Children of Men?"

"All the people in the world are called the Children of Men."

"And were all the people in the world once lost, dear mother?"

"Yes, all mankind were once lost, and about to be destroyed by hungry wolves—

but the Lord saved them, and brought them out of the wilderness."

"Won't you tell us all about it, mother?"

"Yes, if you will listen very attentively. I do not mean that all children of men were lost in just such a wood as Edward and Ellen were lost in; nor, that they were in danger of being eaten up by such wolves as threatened to eat up this dear little boy and girl."

"What kind of wolves were they?" asked the children.

"They were just such things in their hearts as corresponded to wolves and every evil and hurtful beast—wicked passions. But let me tell you all about it. The Lord made men innocent and good. All things around them were as beautiful as the fairest garden you have ever seen. In their hearts dwelt only those good feelings to which the lambs and doves and all good animals correspond. They were very happy, and angels were their companions.

"But, after a while, the children of men

began to forget the good Lord who made them, and gave them every blessing they enjoyed. At the same time that they forgot God, they forgot to love one another. The innocent lambs began to die in their bosoms, and evil beasts of prey to take their place. They hated, instead of loving one another. Then war, dreadful war, first appeared on the earth. Men not only hated, but sought to kill each other. Wicked spirits possessed them, soul and body. They were as if lost in a great wilderness, and about to be destroyed by the wild beasts that were in their hearts.

"It was then that the Lord came and saved them. He drove out the evil spirits and cruel beasts, and led the lost Children of Men out of this dark and fearful wilderness. It was Jesus Christ, of whom you read in the New Testament, the Lord of Heaven and Earth, who did this. When you are older, and can understand better I will tell you more about the lost Children of Men, and the good Lord who saved them."

HARSH WORDS AND KIND WORDS.

"HERE! lend me your knife, Bill; I've left mine in the house," said Edgar Harris to his younger brother. He spoke in a rude voice, and his manner was imperative.

"No, I won't! Go and get your own knife," replied William, in a tone quite as ungracious as that in which the request, or rather command, had been made.

"I don't wish to go into the house. Give me your knife, I say. I only want it for a minute."

"I never lend my knife, nor give it, either," returned William. "Get your own."

"You are the most disobliging fellow I ever saw," retorted Edgar, angrily—rising up and going into the house to get his own knife. "Don't ask me for a favour, for I'll never grant it."

This very unbrotherly conversation took place just beneath the window near which Mr. Harris, the father of the lads, was seated. He overheard it all, and was, as may be supposed, grieved that his sons should treat each other so unkindly. But he said nothing to them then, nor did he let them know that he heard the language which had passed between them.

In a little while Edgar returned, and as he sat down in the place where he had been seated before, he said—

"No thanks to you for your old knife! Keep it to yourself in welcome. I wouldn't use it now, if you were to give it to me."

"I am glad you are so independent,"

retorted William. "I hope you will always be so."

And then the boys fretted each other for some time.

On the next day, Edgar was building a house with sticks, and William was rolling a hoop. By accident, the hoop was turned from its right course, and broke down a part of Edgar's house. William was just going to say how sorry he was for the accident, and to offer to repair the damage that was done, when his brother, with his face red with passion, cried out—

"Just see what you have done! If you don't clear out with your hoop, I'll call father. You did it on purpose."

"Do, go and call him! I'll go with you," said William, in a sneering, tantalizing tone. "Come! come along now."

For a little while the boys stood and growled at each other like two ill-natured dogs, and then Edgar commenced repairing his house, and William went to rolling his hoop again. The latter was strongly tempted to repeat, in earnest, what he had done at first by accident, by way of retaliation upon his brother for his spiteful manner toward him; but being naturally of a good disposition, and forgiving in his temper, he soon forgot his bad feelings, and enjoyed his play as much as he had done before.

This little circumstance Mr. Harris had also observed.

A day or two afterward, Edgar came to his father with a complaint against his brother.

"I never saw such a boy," said he. "He won't do the least thing to oblige me. If I ask him to lend me his knife, or ball, or any thing that he has, he snaps me up short with a refusal."

"Perhaps you don't ask him right," suggested the father. "Perhaps you don't speak kindly to him. I hardly think that William is ill-disposed and disobliging naturally. There must be some fault on your part, I am sure."

"I don't know how I can be in fault, father," said Edgar.

"William refused to let you have his knife the other day, although he was not using it himself, did he not?"

"Yes, sir."

"Do you remember how you asked him for it?"

"No, sir, not now, particularly."

"Well, as I happened to overhear you, I can repeat your words, though I hardly think I can get your very tone and manner. Your words were, 'Here, lend me your knife, Bill;' and your voice and manner were exceedingly offensive. I did not at all wonder that William refused your request. If you had spoken to him in a kind manner, I am sure he would have handed you his knife instantly. But no one likes to be ordered, in a domineering way, to do any thing at all. I know you would resent it in William, as quickly as he resents it in you. Correct your own fault, my son, and in a little while you will have no complaint to make of William."

Edgar felt rebuked. What his father said he saw to be true.

"Whenever you want William to do any thing for you," continued the father, "use kind words instead of harsh ones, and you will find him as obliging as you could wish. I have observed you both a good deal, and I notice that you rarely ever speak to William in a proper manner, but are rude and overbearing. Correct this evil in yourself, and all will be right with him. Kind words are far more powerful than harsh words, and their effect a hundred-fold greater."

On the next day, as Edgar was at work in the garden, and William standing at the gate looking on, Edgar wanted a rake that was in the summer-house. "He was just going to say, "Go and get me that rake, Bill!" but he checked himself, and made his request in a different form, and in a better tone than those words would have been uttered in.

"Won't you get me the small rake that lies in the summer-house, William?" said he. The words and tone involved a request, not a command, and William instantly replied—

"Certainly;" and bounded away to get the rake for his brother.

"Thank you," said Edgar, as he received the rake.

"Don't you want the watering-pot?" asked William.

"Yes, I do; and you may bring it full of water, if you please," was the reply.

Off William went for the watering-pot, and soon returned with it full of water. As he stood near one of Edgar's flower-beds he forgot himself and stepped back with his foot upon some pansies.

"There! just look at you!" exclaimed Edgar, thrown off his guard.

William, who had felt drawn toward his brother on account of his kind manner, was hurt at this sudden change in his words and tone. He was tempted to retort harshly, and even to set his foot more roughly upon the pansies. But he checked himself, and turning away, walked slowly from the garden.

Edgar, who had repented of his rude words and unkind manner the moment he had time to think, was very sorry that he had been thrown off of his guard, and resolved to be more careful in the future. And he was more careful. The next time he spoke to his brother, it was in a kind and gentle manner, and he saw its effect. Since then, he has been watchful over himself, and now he finds that William is one of the most obliging boys anywhere to be found.

"So much for kind words, my son," said his father, on noticing the great change that had taken place. "Never forget, throughout your whole life, that kind words are far more potent than harsh ones. I have found them so and you have already proved the truth of what I say."

And so will every one who tries them. Make the experiment, young friends, and you will find it to succeed in every case.

THE DRUNKARD'S GOOD ANGELS.

"COME, Ady and Jane, it's time you were in bed," said Mrs. Freeman to her two little girls, about nine o'clock one evening. Ady was nine years old, and Jane was a year and a half younger. The two children had been sitting at the work-table with their mother, one of them studying her lesson, and the other engaged on a piece of fancy needlework.

"Papa hasn't come yet," answered Ady.

"No, dear. But it's getting late, and is time you were in bed. He may not be home for an hour."

Ady laid aside her work and left the table, and Jane closed her books and put them away in her school-satchel.

"You can light the little lamp on the mantel-piece," said Mrs. Freeman, after a few minutes, looking around as she spoke, when she saw that the children had both put on their bonnets, and were tying their warm capes close about their necks. She understood very well the meaning of this; and, therefore, did not ask a question, although the tears came to her eyes, and her voice trembled as she said—

"It is very cold out, to-night, children."

"But we won't feel it, mother," replied Ady. "We'll run along very quickly."

And the two little ones went out, before their mother, whose feelings were choking her, could say a word more. As they closed the door after them, and left her alone, she raised her eyes upward, and murmured—

"God bless and reward the dear children!"

It was a bleak, winter night; and, as the little adventurers stepped into the street, the wind swept fiercely along, and almost drove them back against the door. But they caught each other tightly by the hands, and bending their little forms to meet the pressure of the cold, rushing air, hurried on the way they were going as fast as their feet could move. The streets were dark and deserted, but the children were not afraid; love filled their hearts, and left no room for fear.

They did not speak a word to each other as they hastened along. After going for a distance of several blocks, they stopped before a house, over the door of which was a handsome, ornamental gas-lamp, bearing the words "Oysters and Refreshments." It was a strange place for two little girls like them to enter, and at such an hour; but after standing for a moment, they pushed against the green door, which turned lightly on its hinges, and stepped into a large and brilliantly lighted bar-room.

"Bless us!" exclaimed a man, who sat reading at a table. "Here are those babes again!"

Ady and Jane stood still, near the door,

and looked all around the room. But not seeing the object of their search, they went up to the bar, and said timidly to a man who stood behind it, pouring liquor into glasses—

"Has papa been here to-night?"

The man leaned over the bar, until his face was close to the children, when he said, in an angry way,—

"I don't know any thing about your father. And, see here! don't you come here any more. If you do, I'll call my big dog out of the yard and make him bite you."

Ady and Jane felt frightened, as well by the harsh manner as the angry words of the man, and they started back from him, and were turning toward the door with sad faces, when the person who had first remarked their entrance called out, loud enough for them to hear him—

"Come here, my little girls."

The children stopped and looked at him,

when he beckoned for them to approach, and they did so.

"Are you looking for your father?" he asked.

"Yes, sir," replied Ady.

"What did that man at the bar say to you?"

"He said papa wasn't here; and that if we came any more, he would set his dog on us."

"He did!"

"Yes, sir."

The man knit his brows for an instant. Then he said—

"Who sent you here?"

"Nobody," answered Ady.

"Don't your mother know you have come?"

"Yes, sir. She told us to go to bed; but we couldn't go until papa was home. And so we came for him, first."

"He is here!"

"Is he?" And the children's faces brightened.

"Yes. He's at the other side of the room asleep. I'll wake him for you."

Half intoxicated, and sound asleep, it was with some difficulty that Mr. Freeman could be aroused.

As soon, however, as his eyes were fairly opened, and he found that Ady and Jane had each grasped tightly one of his hands, he arose up, and yielding passively to their direction, suffered them to lead him away.

"Oh dear!" exclaimed a man who had looked on with wonder and deep interest. "That's a temperance lecture that I can't stand. God bless the little ones!" he added with emotion, "and give them a sober father."

"I guess you never saw them before?" said one of the bar-keepers lightly.

"No; and I never wish to again; at least in this place. Who is their father?"

"Freeman, the lawyer."

"Not the one who, a few years ago, conducted, with so much ability, the case against the Marine Insurance Company?"

"The same."

"Is it possible?"

A little group now formed around the man, and a good deal was said about Freeman and his fall from sobriety. One who had several times seen Ady and Jane come in, and lead him home as they had just done, spoke of them with much feeling, and all agreed that it was a most touching case.

"To see," said one, "how passively he yields himself to the little things, when they come after him. I feel, sometimes, when I see them, almost weak enough to shed tears."

"They are his good angels," remarked another. "But I'm afraid they are not strong enough to lead him back to the paths he has forsaken."

"You can think what you please about it, gentlemen," spoke up the landlord, "but I can tell you my opinion on the subject: I wouldn't give much for the mother who would let two little things like them go wandering about the street alone, at this time of night."

One of those who had expressed interest in the children, felt angry at this remark, and he retorted with some bitterness—

"And I would give less for the man who would make their father drunk!"

"Ditto to that," responded one of the company.

"And here's my hand to that," said another.

The landlord, finding that the majority of his company were likely to be against him, smothered his angry feelings and kept silence. A few minutes afterward, two or three of the inmates of the bar-room went away.

About ten o'clock on the next morning, while Mr. Freeman, who was generally sober in the fore part of the day, was in his office, a stranger entered, and after sitting down, said—

"I must crave your pardon beforehand

for what I am going to say. Will you promise not to be offended?"

"If you offer me an insult I will resent it," said the lawyer.

"So far from that, I come with the desire to do you a great service."

"Very well. Say on."

"I was at Lawson's refectory last night."

"Well?"

"And I saw something there that touched my heart. If I slept at all last night, it was only to dream of it. I am a father, sir! I have two little girls; and I love them tenderly. Oh, sir! the thought of their coming out, in the cold winter night, in search of me, in such a polluted place, makes the blood feel cold in my veins."

Words so unexpected, coming upon Mr. Freeman when he was comparatively sober, disturbed him deeply. In spite of all his endeavours to remain calm, he trembled all over. He made an effort to say something in reply; but could not utter a word.

"My dear sir," pursued the stranger, "you have fallen at the hand of the monster intemperance, and I feel that I am in great peril. You have not, however, fallen hopelessly. You may yet rise, if you will. Let me, then, in the name of the sweet babes who have shown, in so wonderful a manner, their love for you, conjure you to rise superior to this deadly foe. Reward those dear children with the highest blessing their hearts can desire. Come with me and sign the pledge of freedom. Let us, though strangers to each other, unite in this one good act. Come!"

Half bewildered, yet with a new hope in his heart, Freeman arose, and suffered the man, who drew his arm within his, to lead him away. Before they separated, both had signed the pledge.

That evening, unexpectedly, and to the joy of his family, Mr. Freeman was perfectly sober when he came home. After tea, while Ady and Jane were standing on either side of him, as he sat near their mother, an arm around each of them, he said, in a low whisper, as he bent his head down and drew them closer—

"You will never have to come for me again."

The children lifted their eyes quickly to his face, but half understanding what he meant.

"I will never go there again," he added. "I will always stay at home with you."

Ady and Jane, now comprehending what their father meant, overcome with joy, hid their faces in his lap and wept for very gladness.

Low as all this had been said, every word reached the mother's ear; and while her heart yet stood trembling between hope and fear, Mr. Freeman drew a paper from his pocket and threw it on the table by which she was sitting. She opened it hastily. It was a pledge, with his well-known signature subscribed at the bottom.

With a cry of joy she sprang to his side,

and his arms encircled his wife as well as his little ones, in a fonder embrace than they had known for years.

The children's love had saved their father. They were, indeed, his good angels.

GOOD AND EVIL ANIMALS.

THERE are in the world a great many animals, and all of them correspond to good or evil qualities in men. The good animals are innocent and useful; but the evil animals are cruel and hurtful. Sheep, and cows, and doves are good animals; but wolves, and bears, and hawks are evil animals. Every one loves the gentle lambs that sport in the green fields, but no one likes the cruel wolves that tear these dear lambs in pieces.

In the picture you will see a flock of sheep, with some children and their mo-

and his arms encircled his wife as well as his little ones, in a fonder embrace than they had known for years.

The children's love had saved their father. They were, indeed, his good angels.

GOOD AND EVIL ANIMALS.

THERE are in the world a great many animals, and all of them correspond to good or evil qualities in men. The good animals are innocent and useful; but the evil animals are cruel and hurtful. Sheep, and cows, and doves are good animals; but wolves, and bears, and hawks are evil animals. Every one loves the gentle lambs that sport in the green fields, but no one likes the cruel wolves that tear these dear lambs in pieces.

In the picture you will see a flock of sheep, with some children and their mother gazing at them. How gentle, and innocent, and mild they look! They are safe in the fold where no wicked beasts can harm them. Sometimes a sheep or a lamb will stray from the fold, and then the good shepherd will go off into the woods and mountains to seek the lost one; and when he has found him, he will, if it be a poor little lamb, take him in his arms and carry him back again; or, if a sheep, lead him kindly to the fold from which he had strayed away.

Do you know, dear children, who is your good Shepherd? He is the Lord, and he is ever watching over you, and seeking to protect you from the wolves.

You think there are no wolves to harm you! All evil tempers and bad passions, my children, are wolves; and these, if you let them come into your hearts, will greatly harm, and, perhaps, in the end, destroy you. You stray from this good Shepherd when you indulge in wicked tempers, or do wicked things; and you are then in great danger from the wolves. Keep within the sheep-fold, dear little ones, and your good Shepherd will ever be near to save you from all harm. When you love each other, and seek to make each other happy; when you are obedient to your parents and teachers; then are you within the heavenly sheepfold; then are you safe from the wolves.

THE MOTHER'S GRAVE.

FRANK HARROLD, when he was about twelve years old, got acquainted with some bad boys of his own age. Before this Frank was a very good lad, and gave his mother no trouble. Mrs. Harrold was a very pious woman, and early taught her son that there was a God in heaven, who was to be loved and worshipped by living in obedience to his commands, which were written in the Bible. As soon as he could speak he was taught to say his prayers on going to bed; and when he had learned to read, the Holy Book was oftener in his hands than any other. Mrs. Harrold had great comfort of mind in thinking about her boy; for there was every promise of his growing up to be a good and useful man. He was obedient to her in all things, and kind to his playmates; and never seemed so happy as when he could oblige some one.

But, as we have said, when Frank was about twelve years old, he got into the company of bad boys, who enticed him away into evil. It was sad to see the change that soon passed over him. He learned to use bad language: that is, low, obscene, and profane language; such as may be heard from the gangs of vicious boys, to be seen congregated at particular times, in all our towns or large cities. From being kind to others, he soon learned to feel pleasure in giving pain through direct personal injury, by ridicule, or by wounding the feelings of those weaker than himself.

Alas! how quickly do the angels go away from us, when, by our evil thoughts and acts, we associate our minds with evil spirits, who ever stand waiting to flow in upon us and rule our lives. If we would keep out these enemies, we must keep our thoughts pure, and guard our lips as we would guard a precious treasure in a golden casket. Bad language does not correspond to any thing in heaven; it only corresponds to something evil in hell. When a boy, therefore, swears, or uses any kind of obscene or bad language, the evil spirits who are always trying to enter his mind, perceive something that is congenial to themselves, and come in. Immediately on this occurring, the good angels, who cannot occupy the same habitation with evil spirits, retire, and then the boy is more under the influence of evil than of good. The only way to cast them out again, and bring back those other and better companions, is to refrain from evil speaking of any kind, and also to push away evil thoughts, when the angels will return and fill the mind with their own pure thoughts and peaceful feelings. It is the same when a boy gets angry with his companions, or when he permits himself to have covetous thoughts, or tells a lie, or does or thinks any thing that is evil. The moment this takes place, there is a change. Evil spirits perceive their own, and flow into it, while the good angels are cast out. Only in what is good in the mind, can the latter abide; and when good is removed, they must go with it.

If this is understood by the thoughtful young reader, he will see how important it is for him to watch over his temper and guard his lips. Let him not, as he values his best interests, give way to any wrong desire, indulge in any bad temper, or use any but pure and innocent language. If he so watch over his thoughts, words, and actions, and look for help from above, he need be in no fear of evil, for it cannot reach him.

But Frank Harrold did not thus guard himself. He thought, when he heard boys of his own age swear, and saw them smoke disgusting cigars, and drink drams, that all this was manly. At first, he felt such an inward reluctance—such a painful drawing back—when he made an attempt to swear, in imitation of his bad companions, that he could not utter the word that was in his thoughts. But, after a while, he forced out a wicked oath; and then it all came easy enough. Swearing led to other and worse vices; and so the feet of the poor lad, having once entered an evil way, began to move in it swiftly.

Mrs. Harrold was deeply distressed at this sad change in her boy, and did every thing in her power to win him away from his dangerous companions. But their power over him was so great, that all she said made little or no impression upon his mind. At last, when she talked to him, he would get angry, and speak unkindly to his good mother; and even though tears would come into her eyes when he did so, not the least movement of repentance or pity was in his heart.

And so it went on. The lad grew worse and worse; and, when he was eighteen years old, had become so debased in his conduct, and so idle in his habits, that no one would have him in his employ. About this time a recruiting-sergeant came into the town, and Frank, when half intoxicated, was induced to enlist as a soldier for a term of five years. He felt bad enough when he became fully sober, and reflected upon what he had done. But repentance was now too late. As for his mother, she was almost heart-broken.

In a few weeks, Frank was sent off to the frontier, among the Indians, where, for five years, he endured various hardships, and lived among people of the worst class. As a common soldier, he was tyrannized over by petty officers, and made to suffer indignities and degradation worse than is endured by many slaves at the South. And for all this, his pay was no more than the hired domestic in his mother's house had regularly received. Once he was thrown from a horse, while riding in a troop over a prairie, and had his leg broken; once he was shot in the knee by an Indian; and the wound, from which he suffered dreadful pain, kept him in the hospital attached to the barracks for two or three months. Exposed in all weathers, in a sickly region, he was frequently ill with raging fevers. But, when bowed in pain and sickness, there was no gentle mother's hand to make smooth his pillow, and no mother's voice to speak loving words in his ears. The hospital nurse was a rough soldier, and the physician of the regiment a cruel tyrant, who could safely exercise his overbearing spirit on poor sick dragoons, that dared not resent his outrages and indignities. Ah! it was all very different from what it would have been, had Frank grown up an industrious, obedient, and good boy. Thus it is, that evil ever brings its own punishment. Frank, while lying sick, used to think of all this; and such thoughts always made his heart ache.

A year before the soldier's term of service expired, news came to him that his mother was dead. Oh! how he wept over this sad intelligence. How bitterly he repented of the evil into which he had fallen; and by which not only his own life, but that of his excellent mother, had been rendered miserable!

"I have killed her!" he murmured, as his eyes grew dim, and he could not see the lines of writing in the letter that conveyed the afflicting news. From the day Frank received this letter, until his term of service expired, no one saw him smile. On receiving his discharge, he returned, as quickly as he could come, to his native village. But he did not go among the people, nor seek out old friends, nor search for employment. He went to the graveyard, where, by the side of the green mound of earth that had covered for many years the mouldering ashes of his father,

he found that another had been buried—
and knew the fresh-made grave as the one
which contained the earthly remains of his
mother. For hours he sat here and wept.
Then he went from the little enclosure,
feeling, as he did so, that he was an out-
cast in the world. Despairing thoughts
began to arise, and evil suggestions were
flowing into his mind. But, amid these,
arose the image of his mother; and then
his thoughts went back to the time when,
a little child, he knelt beside her, and
prayed that he might not be led into
temptation. So softened were his feelings,
that, sinking upon his knee, he clasped his
hands, and prayed aloud, as his heart went
upward—

"Lead me not into temptation!"

And as he did so, there came a light
into his heart, and a good purpose formed
in his mind.

"I have had enough of this evil life," he
said; "it brings nothing but suffering.
Dear mother in heaven! draw near thy

unhappy child! Be to him a good angel, as thou wert in the early days of childhood and innocence."

After saying this, the young man arose, and returning to the grave of his mother, sat there again and wept. But the shadows of evening, that soon began to fall, warned him that he must retire; and then he went away, firm in his purpose to lead a new life.

Glad are we to say, that this good purpose was never broken, and that Frank Harrold is now a sober, industrious young man; engaged in useful employments, and as happy as could be expected for one who must have so many painful memories.

Dear children! Give not a moment's place to evil in your minds; for evil is a cruel tyrant, and leads into the worst slavery, and the most direful sufferings, all who give themselves up to its influence. Only the good are happy.

THE STORY OF A LITTLE LAMB.

"GET a book and read me a pretty story," said little Anna to her sister Jane.

"Shall I read to you about the lamb that was lost, and came near dying?"

"And heard the tinkling of a distant sheep-bell?"

"Yes."

"Oh yes, sister Jane, read me that pretty story. I love to hear it."

So Jane took up a book in which the story was printed, and read to Anna about the little lamb.

"It was on a soft morning in May, when a certain little lamb was called from sleep by the tinkling of the sheep-bell. Slowly he raised his head, still keeping his forefeet bent under his bosom, and looked with a sleepy eye after his mother, who had just trotted away from his side. Again the bell sounded, and the pretty little lamb rose upon his feet, and was soon leaping by his mother's side. Now, the field in which these sheep dwelt was a place of great beauty; the verdant hill, the sparkling streamlet, the shady tree, the green pasture, were all there; it seemed a quiet fold apart from the rest of the world—a pleasant place on purpose for that happy little flock. Now, the little lamb of which I have been speaking was the darling of the flock; no other had so white a fleece, so mild an eye, so gentle a nature. One day, as this little lamb was playing by himself, at a short distance from the fold, he was espied by an eagle, who no sooner beheld him than he darted down, and, seizing him in his talons, bore him far away from the little flock. Oh! it was sad to see the sheep look after their darling lamb; and the poor little lamb once caught the distant tinkling of the sweet bell it had so loved to follow. Now, as the eagle was flying over a valley, an archer shot an arrow which went into its heart, and it fell with the lamb at the archer's feet. Then the archer took the lamb home to his child, and bade him take care of the poor little creature. Now the child had a tender heart, and he took the lamb, and bathed its wounds, and washed the blood from its snowy fleece, and wept. But the lamb began to revive, and the child was glad: and he took a silken cord and placed it about his neck, and led the lamb about with him wherever he went; and in the joy of his heart he thought the lamb must be as happy as himself. But it pined for the loss of its mother's love, and the peace it had known amid the happy little flock in the far-off fold. One summer day, the child, being weary with long rambling, fell asleep on a bank of flowers, still holding the silken cord tightly in his hand; but looser and looser it became, till it slipped away from his grasp, and the little lamb fled away from him for ever.

"Onward and onward went the lamb, not knowing whither. After a time it began to rain, and the thunder rolled and the lightning flashed. The poor little lamb trembled; but when the thunder was not heard for a moment, he forgot his sorrows, and stopped to nibble a daisy; then, startled by a sudden flash, he looked up in terror, and was again driven onward by the loud-pealing thunder. On he went, over a wide common, till he came to the foot of a steep hill, which, with weary feet, he climbed; but when he had gained the summit, weak and trembling, he laid down to die; his eyes became dim, and his heart beat faintly in his bosom: but the thought of his mother and the peaceful fold, the sweet flowers, and all things he had loved in the first happy moments of his little life were present to his eye: and the poor lamb closed his eyes in sorrow.

"But as his heart grew more faint, he was startled by the tinkling of a distant bell; and slowly raising his head, he beheld his own little flock in their own happy fold; and new life awoke in his heart, and new light shone from his eyes, and new strength came to his feet, and in a moment more the lost lamb was by his mother's side, telling how he had been called back to life by the tinkling of that sweet sheep-bell."

THE YOUNG TEACHER.

"I WISH I knew how to read!" said one little boy to another.

"Then why don't you learn?" asked his companion.

"Because I have no one to teach me, and my mother is too poor to send me to school," replied the boy.

The name of the little boy who could read was Albert Parker, and the name of the one who could not read was Henry Morrison.

"I think I could teach you," said Albert.

"Do you? Oh, I wish you would try, for I want to learn to read very much."

The earnestness with which Henry spoke made Albert resolve that he would at least try, although, as he was but a small boy, and had only just learned to read himself, he did not feel certain that he could teach Henry; but, then, he determined in his own mind, young as he was, that he would make the trial.

"Do you know your A, B, C's?" asked Albert.

"Oh yes. I can say them all through."

"Will you come into our house now, and try to learn? I have got all my books there."

Of course Henry consented, and the two boys went into the house, and sat down on two little chairs, that Albert's mother gave them to sit on, when she learned her son's kind intentions. She felt very glad to see him, so early in life, in the effort to do good; for she was a woman who loved the Lord and her neighbour, and had taught her boy that it was right for him to try and do the same. She looked on and listened, with a heart full of pleasure, to the young teacher and his pupil.

Albert. You know all your A, B, C's?

Henry. Yes; I know every one of them.

A. Then you must learn your A-b ab's next.

H. Well, where are they?

A. (Turning over the leaves of one of his little books.) Here they are. Now begin. What letter is that?

H. A.

A. And the little one alongside of it?

H. B.

A. Well; A-b spells ab. Now what letter is that?

H. E.

A. And the little one?

H. B.

A. That spells eb. And this i-b ib, o-b ob, and u-b ub. Now try and see if you can say the whole line?

H. A-b—

A. Ab.

H. Oh yes; A-b ab, e-b eb, i-b ib, o-b ob, u-b ub.

A. Yes; that is all right. Why, how fast you learn! Now go over it again.

And Henry commenced the lesson and went all through it, without missing a single one of the little words. Then Albert tried him in his B-a ba's, and soon he could say all of these. For an hour the little boys were all intent, the one in teaching and the other in learning. At the end of this time, Henry could give the true sound of all the words of two letters in the primer.

Albert's mother had been attentive to all that passed, as she sat engaged in sewing, and when the little boys laid aside their book, she said—

"You must come here every day, Henry, and let Albert teach you to read."

Henry promised that he would come, and then the little boys went out and played until it was time for Henry to go home.

On the next day, after Albert had returned from school, Henry Morrison came again, and took another lesson. And so he continued coming every day. At the end of a week he could spell out some of the easy lines that were in the first reading-book, such as—

"My son, go not in the way of bad men."

Now Albert's father, when he saw that Henry Morrison was so eager to learn, thought within himself that he would send him to school. So, after he had been to see, and had talked with his mother, who promised to keep him always clean, and his clothes neatly mended, he entered him at the same school to which his own son went.

The reason why Mr. Parker was willing to place Henry at the same school to which his own son was going, was because he saw that Henry was a good boy; that he never said bad words, nor had any bad habits. He was not, therefore, afraid to let his own son be in company with him.

You may suppose that Henry Morrison learned very fast at school. And so he did. In a few months he caught up to Albert and soon went rapidly past him. But it is pleasing to be able to say, that Albert Parker had not a single unkind or envious feeling toward Henry on this account, but was, on the contrary, exceedingly pleased.

"How is it, Albert," his father said to him one day, "that Henry learns so much faster than you do?"

Albert thought, at first, that this question was meant for a rebuke, but when he looked up into his father's face, he saw that it was not.

"I don't know how it is, father," he answered, "but he can and does learn faster than I can, and I am glad of it."

"Glad of it, Albert! And why so?"

"Why, you know, father, that Henry

can't go to school as long as I can, and so he ought to learn a great deal faster. I shall be learning on still when he has to be put out to a trade, to get his own living."

"And so you do not envy him, because he learns so much faster than you do?"

"Oh no, father; why should I? It would be wicked in me, would it not?"

"Certainly, my son. And I am glad to hear you say that you are pleased to see your little friend learn faster than you can. Still, you must try your best."

"And so I do, father. And I learn as fast as any boy in my class. But the schoolmaster says that Henry is the fastest boy in the whole school."

For three years Mr. Parker continued to send Henry to school, after which it became necessary for him to go out to a trade, as his poor mother could not support him any longer. When he left the school, he was far in advance of all the other scholars, and his desire to learn was still greater than it had ever been.

He felt very grateful to Mr. Parker, and, before he went to his trade, came and thanked him for his great kindness to him. While the poor boy thus expressed his gratitude, Mr. Parker felt doubly repaid for all he had done.

"You are now far in advance, Henry, of most boys when they go to a trade," said he, "and if you will only employ your spare time in improving yourself, you may rise high in the world, and be very useful when you grow up to be a man. Some of the best and greatest men in the country, when boys, were poor like you, and had to work at trades. Persevere, then, as they did, and you will rise as high. But above all, Henry, ever remember that you are in the presence of the good and holy Lord, who cannot look upon sin with the least degree of allowance. Let His commandments be ever before you. Do not break the least one of them wilfully; for, if you do, unhappiness will surely follow. And now, my boy," his kind benefactor added fervently, "may our Heavenly Father ever have you in his holy keeping."

Throughout his whole life Henry Morrison did not forget the impression of that moment. As an apprentice, instead of wasting, as too many boys do, their leisure time in idleness, his books were always resorted to, and some information gained at every spare moment. Still, he was careful never to neglect his work, nor to hurry through it so as not to do it well. This his master, who was a kind man, saw, and he therefore took pleasure in seeing him at his books, when his work was done.

Albert continued to be the friend of Henry. They met every Sabbath at the Sunday-school, and frequently the latter would go home and spend the evening in Mr. Parker's family.

Thus he continued to improve his mind, until he arrived at the age of manhood, when, his mother having died several years before, he removed many hundred miles away from his native place.

It was about ten years afterward that Albert Parker was travelling in the West, and stopped a few days at Louisville, Kentucky.

He attended church on the Sabbath-day, as was his custom, whether at home or abroad; for the pious instructions received in early life had been like good seed sown upon good ground.

When the minister arose in the pulpit, there seemed to Albert something strangely familiar in his face and form; but when he spoke, his voice sounded like that of an old friend.

"Surely I have seen him before," said he, as he looked at him earnestly, and tried to remember where and when he had met with him. But he could recall neither the time, the place, nor the circumstance.

He listened to the sermon with the deepest attention. It was full of true and beautiful thoughts, and the style and language were eloquent and imposing. His text was—

"*Cast thy bread upon the waters: for thou shalt find it after many days.*"—Eccles. xi. 1.

In closing, he said—"I will give you a practical illustration of what I have been trying to impress upon your minds. Two little boys, about ten years of age, were playing together. One of them was a poor boy, and could not read. Young as he was, he felt an anxious desire to learn like other boys, but his mother was poor, and could not send him to school. 'I wish I could read!' said he, to his companion. 'Then why don't you learn?' asked the other little boy; and he replied, 'Because I have no one to teach me, and my mother is too poor to send me to school.' Then the boy who could read said, that 'he thought he could teach him, and if the other were willing he would try.' Of course he was willing, and the two little boys sat down together, one as teacher and the other as scholar, and while the one endeavoured to impart the little that he had learned, the other tried as hard to receive what his young friend so earnestly endeavoured to give. And in this way the poor boy learned to read. The father of his little friend, on seeing him so anxious to learn, sent him to school for three years. That poor boy, in the providence of the Lord, is now your minister. His kind teacher he has neither seen nor heard from for many years, but he yet hopes to meet him. The bread cast, more than twenty years ago, upon the waters, he will yet find."

As soon as the minister began to speak of that early scene, the countenance of Henry Morrison grew at once familiar to Albert Parker. Their meeting after service was indeed a joyful one. Tears moistened their eyes, as they grasped each other's hands and uttered their heartfelt expressions of delight.

Years have passed since that pleasant interview, and both are now ministers, eminent for talents and usefulness.

THE LITTLE BOY AND HIS MOTHER.

Page 69.

A CONVERSATION.

"WHEN sister was ill, and you were so sorry, mother, why did you not pray to God?—would he not have made her well?"

"Perhaps not, my child."

"Why, mother, would not God have heard your prayer?"

"Yes, but he might not have seen fit to grant such a prayer, if I had been disposed to make it."

"If you had been disposed to make it! Mother, did you not wish that sister might get well?"

"Certainly I wished it; but I wish still more that what God sees will be best for me, and for those I love, may happen,—because I know that God is ever striving to do us every possible good, and he might have known that it would not have been either for my real good, or your sister's, to grant such a prayer. Why did I not give you the cake which you wished for yesterday?"

"Because you thought it would make me sick."

"And yet you wished very much for the cake. And you know that I love you, and would like to grant you any enjoyment that is good for you; but you do not know so well as I do, that to grant some of your wishes would be hurtful to you. Now, God watches over our spiritual health and happiness, with far more love and care than that with which the tenderest parents watch over their children. He knows and grants what he sees will promote these, and he withholds that only which he knows would do us harm. Remember, then, my dear little boy, that the Lord knows what is good for us, and is always ready to give it. Our prayers are needful, therefore, only to make us feel and acknowledge our constant dependence upon him, and to express our grateful sense of his continual goodness and our humble submission to his will."

SPEAK KINDLY.

THOUGH intemperate, and at times idle, Mr. Marker had not wholly given himself up to the evil of drinking. He worked pretty regularly at his trade, and gave the greater part of his earnings to his wife. But he spent at least a dollar and a half a week in liquor, and sometimes more. This sum, added to what might have been earned in the time lost in consequence of intemperate habits, shows a good deal of money wasted, which, if spent in his family, would have given them many comforts.

In consequence of this, poor Mrs. Marker had to work harder and harder every day;

and yet their comforts diminished instead of increasing. Not possessing naturally much evenness of temper, nor a great deal of fortitude, she was, at times, very impatient and fretful; and she became, in the end, so much worried by her husband's conduct, that she hardly ever gave him a pleasant word when he was in the house, and was often the cause of his going out and spending evenings in the taverns when he felt inclined to remain at home.

Mary, their oldest child, was, at the time of which we are writing, just eleven years of age. She loved her father very much, notwithstanding his evil ways; and it often caused her to go off by herself alone, and cry, when angry words passed between him and her mother.

One evening, Mr. Marker brought a book home for Mary, which was received by her with great joy. But she had scarcely taken it in her hand, before her mother said fretfully—

"What's that?"

"Its a book that papa has bought me," replied Mary, holding up her present.

"He must have plenty of money to throw away," said the mother ill-naturedly, for she never could let any opportunity that presented itself pass without saying something that was unkind to her husband. A man who has been drinking is never entirely rational; and as Mr. Marker had poured two or three glasses of fiery liquid down his throat, he was not, of course, in a fit state for reason and self-control. As usual on such occasions, he had something to say in return, and one remark followed another, until there was a war of words. So soon as this had subsided, the unhappy family went to supper, but none of them could eat with any relish. After they had left the table, Mr. Marker, in sitting down for the purpose of reading, happened to say something that his wife thought silly—and men, after they have been drinking, generally talk silly enough—when she said to him—

"Do hush, will you! I hate to hear any one talk like a fool!"

Mary was never happier than when her father remained at home during the evening; and if her mother had taken half the pains to induce him to do so, that she did, he would have been with them four or five evenings every week, instead of in the grog-shop, as was generally the case.

Poor child! How sad she felt when she saw her father throw down his paper and go angrily from the house.

"If mother would only be kind to him," she said to herself, "I am sure he would do better."

The little present he had brought her showed the affection that was in his heart for Mary, debased as it was, and the child's feelings were affected with more than a usual tenderness by the token. The stroke of a lash upon her back could not have hurt her half so much as did the angry words uttered by her mother, and when she saw their effect in fairly driving her father from the house, she could not refrain from weeping. The book, which she had hoped to enjoy for an hour, was laid away out of sight, and she shrank into a corner of the room with a heavy weight of grief on her young heart. All her thoughts were with her father. She knew where he had gone, and was, alas! too well assured that when he came home he would be so much intoxicated as scarcely to be conscious of any thing.

Mrs. Marker was often sorry for her unguarded and ill-chosen words, after she saw the effect of them. It was so on this occasion. Poor woman! how heavily did she sigh as she sat down with her sewing, after having put the supper things away. The effect of her words had been too marked not to leave a feeling of self-condemnation; and this feeling is, perhaps, of all others, most painful to bear.

Mr. Marker had been gone only a few minutes, when Mary arose and left the room. Upon a chair in the passage lay an old shawl, which she threw over her head, and then glided noiselessly from the house.

The night was cold, and Mary shivered when the heavy air first struck upon her thinly-clad form. But she soon forgot the wintry atmosphere through which she was passing. A few blocks away, was one of those man-traps, called refectories, into which, if any one goes, he is in great danger of being ruined both in body and soul. To this place Mary knew that her father went often, and thither she directed her rapid steps. A brilliant gas-lamp burned just in front of the refectory, and there was a beautiful transparency in the window. Without, all looked attractive; and there was a promise of good cheer within to tempt the unwary. Before the door Mary stood for a few moments, and then entered, stealthily, like one who felt that her presence would be unwelcome.

Mr. Marker, on leaving home, felt very much fretted in his temper. Something had occurred during the day to cause him to reflect; and the consequence was, that he had indulged his appetite for drink less frequently than usual. When he returned to his family in the evening, although he had been drinking, he was nearer to being a sober man than he had been for weeks. This, unfortunately, his wife did not perceive, and her harsh language came, therefore, upon certain good resolutions, like wind upon the chaff, and scattered them in the air.

On going from the house in a passion, Mr. Marker went, as his little daughter had supposed, to the refectory. On entering, he called for a glass of ale, and taking it to a table, sat down with a newspaper in his hand. After taking a draught of the liquor, he commenced reading. But he found little, if any thing, to interest him. His mind was disturbed; and there was a picture in his imagination, that, if possible, he would have shut out—a picture of home; but he could not. The pleasure that lit up Mary's face, when he gave her the book he had bought, he saw instantly fade before the unkindly spoken word of her mother, and with a certain bitterness of feeling he clenched his hands uneasily and set his teeth tightly together. But, even while he blamed his wife for her fretful temper, thoughts of his own evil doings and their consequences upon his family, came forcing themselves into his mind, and his feelings smarted under the self-accusations of his own conscience. He had, after running his eye hurriedly over the newspaper, reading a line here and there, but not perceiving any meaning in what he read, thrown it down, and was just lifting his glass to take another draught of ale, when he saw Mary enter the door and look timidly around. The glass, before it reached his lips, was returned to the table: so much surprised was he at the appearance of his child in such a place.

It was a moment or two before Mary saw her father; but as soon as her eyes rested upon him, she went quickly over to where he sat, and taking hold of his hand, said, in a low but very tender voice—

"Come, papa!"

Against angry words, the spirit of the man had instantly rebelled; but his heart turned toward his child with her loving gentle tones, and, as if led by an angel from amidst a company of evil spirits, he arose and followed her out into the pure cold air.

Still holding tightly the hand of her father, Mary moved on toward their home, and he walked by her side as passively as if no will of his own remained.

When they reached their cheerless dwelling, both entered, side by side. Mrs. Marker, who, until that moment, was not aware that Mary had left the house, looked up from her work with surprise. She was about saying something, when Mary sprang toward her and whispered in her ear, in an earnest, imploring voice, yet so distinctly, that her father heard her words—"Oh, mamma—speak kindly!"

Mrs. Marker's form drooped over her work, as if nearly all strength had left her. Her face bent low to her needle, but still, for the gathering tears, she could not see. Her husband sat down at a short distance from her, feeling very strange. For a few minutes all was silent. Suddenly Mrs. Marker let her sewing fall from her hands, and rising up, went over to where her husband sat with his eyes upon the floor.

"Edward," she said, in a low, serious voice, "do what you will, I'll never speak unkindly again."

"And I'll never drink another drop!" he replied in an animated voice, springing to his feet.

In a moment they were in each other's arms, and, in tears, gave pledges for a new and a better life.

Oh! it was a joyful time for Mary. She scarcely slept that night for thinking of the happy days that were to come. And she has not been disappointed. Mr. Marker signed the temperance-pledge on the very next day, and faithfully has he kept it since. Than his, few happier homes are now to be found; and no one in that house is happier than Mary.

Oh! there is a wonderful power in kind words.

I CAN'T DO IT.

"I CAN'T do it!" said Henry Bradford, throwing down his pen and dividers, and exhibiting other signs of impatience.

This happened at school, and the teacher's eyes were upon Henry at the time, although the boy did not know it.

"Can't do what, Henry?" asked the teacher, calling to the lad across the school-room.

"Can't work out this problem, sir," replied the lad, looking confused.

"Have you tried to do it?"

"Yes, sir."

"How long have you tried?"

"I've been trying for an hour, sir."

"Bring it to me and let me see what you are doing."

The boy left his seat and came up as directed. After the teacher had looked over his work for a few minutes, he said—

"You must try again, Henry. You have gone the right way about it, but you have made an error in your calculations."

The boy went back to his seat, saying to himself, as he did so, "Its no use to try—I can't do it."

But he knew that he must follow the direction of his teacher, and so he sat down and commenced going over all the calculations again; he had not been more than ten minutes at this before he discovered where the error lay.

"Never say 'I can't do it,' again, Henry," said his teacher, when he took him up the problem accurately worked out. "The boy who says that often is never worth much as a man."

When Henry went home he told his father what the teacher had said.

"He spoke the truth, my son," remarked Mr. Bradford. "I remember a lad who, when he was about your age, had so little confidence in himself that he was discouraged at any and every thing requiring effort. He was always saying, just as you are, 'I can't do it.' And yet, like you, he had as good abilities as most boys."

"Was he never worth much as a man?" asked Henry, innocently.

Mr. Bradford smiled, and said—

"Oh yes. He did very well as a man; but he was cured of his want of confidence in his own abilities before he became a man, or I doubt if he would have turned out good for much."

"How was he cured, father?"

"I will tell you; and I hope you will profit by what I am going to relate. This lad's name was Henry. One day, when he was only fifteen years of age, his father said to him—

"'Henry, my business has got so bad that I am compelled to send away my clerk. You have been going to school for a good many years, and have studied book-keeping, and I suppose can take charge of my books very well. I must take you from school and make you my clerk.'

"'I can't do it indeed,' replied the lad, frightened at the very idea.

"'Oh yes, you can,' answered his father. 'To-morrow you must begin, as William leaves me to-day.'

"On the next morning Henry went to his father's store. When he was shown the huge ledger and journal, also the day-book, bill-book, cash-cook, sales-book, &c., he felt sure that he could not keep them, and said, as he was always in the habit of doing, when any difficulty presented itself: 'I can't do it.'

"'Yes, but I tell you that you can do it, and you must do it,' answered the father, a good deal out of patience with him. 'Try! you can do that, at least.'

"The boy never liked to have his father

displeased with him: he looked up into his face and replied—

"'I will try, father; but I'——

"'We don't want any "but's" about it, Henry,' he said quickly. 'Try—try—try—always be ready to try to do any thing, and you will soon be able to do almost every thing.'

"As Henry's father was so much in earnest about the matter, he had nothing to do but to try. To his own delight and astonishment, before a week had passed he understood the books so well that he could make all the first entries, and carry every thing through to the ledger.

"'You see what can be done by trying,' said his father to him.

"'Yes, sir; but indeed I didn't think I could do it. It looked so hard.'

"'Every thing looks hard that you don't know how to do, my son. But never say you can't do any thing, until you have tried. It will be very strange if you say it afterward.'

"Henry continued to keep his father's books, and to assist him in his business, which improved very much in the course of a couple of years. At the end of this time his father said to him—

"'Henry, I want you to go out to South America with a cargo of flour, in the brig Mary, which I have just purchased.'

"Henry shrank back at the thought. He knew nothing of South America, nor of the manner of doing business there. He had never studied the Spanish language. In fact, he felt himself totally unfitted to go. But his father wouldn't hear a word of objection.

"'I don't know the language,' said Henry.

"'The vessel won't be ready for a month,' was the reply; 'study Spanish during that time.'

"'But I can't acquire a knowledge of the Spanish language in a month,' he replied.

"'Try, try, try, Henry! Don't say

"can't" to any thing. Learn all you can, and then study the language for yourself on the outward voyage, and spend as much time as possible in conversing with the captain, who speaks Spanish very well. My word for it, by the time you reach Rio you will be able to speak enough of the language to answer every purpose.'

"Henry commenced taking lessons in Spanish immediately, and informed himself as minutely as possible about the manner of trading in South America. By the time the vessel sailed, he felt a good deal more confidence in himself. When he arrived on the coast, he found no difficulty whatever in carrying out the purposes of the voyage. It was just as easy, almost, as posting his father's books after he had learned how to do it.

"'I'll never say "I can't do it," again,' he said to his father on returning home. 'I believe I can do almost any thing, if I try.'

"'And so you can, my son. It isn't so

much the want of ability that keeps men from accomplishing great things, as the want of confidence and energy. Be ready to attempt any thing that comes in your way to do, and never say, "I can't do it;" at least, not until you have tried.'

"Henry was as good as his word. From that time he never permitted any difficulty to discourage him, and many and many a one he has had to encounter and overcome. He is now a man, and has a son who is just as easily disheartened as he once was, and who, if he does not overcome this disposition, will never be as successful in the world as his father has been."

"Why, father! It wasn't you, was it?" exclaimed Henry in surprise.

"Yes, my son. I have told you my own history. I was just such a boy as you are, and I was always saying, 'I can't do it,' whenever I encountered any little difficulty. But I learned that all I had to do was to try, and I could do any thing.

And if you ever expect to make a man, you must *try*."

" I *will* try, father," said Henry, inspired with a determination to conquer his weakness. And he did try, and gradually learned that a little perseverance would enable him to overcome almost any difficulty, no matter how discouraging it was at first to look upon.

A GENTLEMAN.

"BE very gentle with her, my son," said Mrs. Butler, as she tied on her little girl's bonnet, and sent her out to play with her elder brother.

They had not been out very long before a cry was heard, and presently Julius came in and threw down his hat, saying—

"I hate playing with girls! There's no fun with them; they cry in a minute."

"What have you been doing to your sister? I see her lying there on the gravel walk: you have torn her frock and pushed her down. I am afraid you forgot my caution to be gentle."

"Gentle! Boys can't be gentle, mother;

its their nature to be rough, and hardy, and boisterous. They are the stuff soldiers and sailors are made of. Its very well to talk of a gentle girl; but a gentle boy—it sounds ridiculous! I should be ready to knock a fellow down for calling me so!"

"And yet, Julius, you would be very angry, a few years hence, if any one were to say you were not a gentle man."

"A gentle man. I never thought of dividing the word in that way before. Being gentle always seems to me like being weak and womanish."

"This is so far from being the case, my son, that you will always find that the bravest men are the most gentle. The spirit of chivalry that you so much admire, was a spirit of the noblest courage and the utmost gentleness combined. Still I dare say you would rather be called a manly than a gentle boy?"

"Yes, indeed, mother."

"Well, then, my son, it is my greatest wish that you should endeavour to unite the two. Show yourself manly when you are exposed to danger or see others in peril; be manly when called on to speak the truth, though the speaking of it may bring reproach upon you; be manly when you are in sickness and pain. At the same time be gentle, whether you be with females or with men; be gentle toward all men. By putting the two qualities together, you will deserve a name which, perhaps, you will not so greatly object to."

"I see what you mean dear mother, and I will endeavour to be what you wish—a gentlemanly boy."

THE LITTLE BOY WHO DIDN'T WANT TO GO TO SABBATH-SCHOOL.
Page 97.

THE SABBATH-SCHOOL.

"I WISH I didn't have to go to Sunday-school," said Harry Sandford to his mother, as she was pinning on his clean collar, and brushing his hair nicely, one bright Sabbath afternoon.

"Would you rather stay at home?" asked his mother.

"Oh yes. A great deal rather."

"Would you play all the time?"

"I would play some, and read some, and do a good many things. I think it is enough to go to school all the week."

"But to-day is Sunday. It is the Lord's day. What does that commandment say which speaks of the Sabbath?"

"It says, 'Six days shalt thou labour and do all thy work, but the seventh day is the Sabbath of the Lord thy God. In it, thou shalt not do any work, thou, nor thy man-servant, nor thy maid-servant, thy ox, nor thy ass, nor thy stranger that is within thy gates. For in six days the Lord made the heavens and the earth, the sea, and all that in them is, and rested on the seventh day; wherefore the Lord blessed the Sabbath-day and hallowed it.'"

"What do you think this means, my son?"

"It means that we mustn't work on Sunday, doesn't it?"

"It means, that on the Lord's holy day we should rest from all worldly employments, and raise our thoughts to heavenly things. The Lord gives us six days in which to labour and do all our natural work, and then the Sabbath comes; the Sabbath, in which our hands are no longer required to labour, nor our thoughts to be engaged in worldly things. On this blessed

THE SABBATH-SCHOOL.

day we can lift up our minds and think about the Lord, and meet together to worship him, and return him our thanks for the many blessings that we receive from him. Now, you, my son, have many hours, each day of the week, for playing, and reading your pretty books. Should you not, then, on the Sabbath, not only be willing but glad to go to Sunday-school, where, with other little children, you can read and hear about the Lord and heaven, and learn to love one another? I know that this will be much better for you."

"But the commandment doesn't say that little boys must go to Sunday-school," said Harry. "I am sure I can rest from labour as well by staying at home."

"Do you believe you will think as much about the Lord and be as thankful to him for all his blessings?"

"Yes, ma'am. I can read in the Bible the same as I do at school."

"And chant and sing hymns of praise to the Lord?"

Little Harry's eyes dropped to the floor.

"And see your kind teacher's face, and hear all the excellent things she says to the children, and love her as well?" continued the mother.

"I can't do all that, I know," returned the boy.

"I know you cannot, my son. Now think. Do you not know, that when you are in company with many persons, you soon get interested in what they are all doing and saying; but that while you are by yourself, you cannot remain long interested in any thing, nor will your interest be as strong as it would be if others shared the pleasure with you. Is not this so? Think."

"I never like to read to myself as well as I do aloud for you to hear," said the boy.

"Nor to play by yourself as well as you do with other children?"

"Oh no, ma'am."

"Nor would you be able to keep the commandment, 'Remember the Sabbath-day to keep it holy,' as well alone, as if you were associated with other little boys and girls, met together for the same purpose. Do you *now* think that you would?"

"I am afraid not, mother."

"I am sure that you would not, Henry. And it is for this reason that your father and mother wish you to go to the Sabbath-school. It is for this reason that your teachers meet with you every Sabbath. They know that they can do you good when you are all together and they can see you and talk to you face to face."

"I don't want to stay at home now," said little Harry, putting his arms around his mother's neck and kissing her. "I will go to the Sabbath-school, for I know it will be better for me."

"And not only better for you, my son," said the mother. "It will be better for the other little boys and girls. Think of that!"

"Why, how can that be, mother?"

"If the company of others helps you to think of the Lord and his goodness, your company will help them to do the same. You all help each other. For the sake of other little boys and girls, then, it is your duty to go to school. Your presence adds one to the company, and makes it stronger. If you stay away, and another and another stay away, the few who are left will not find the school so pleasant, nor be able, while there, to take so much delight in reading the word, and singing in praise of the Lord's goodness. For the sake of others, then, as well as yourself, my dear boy, you must go regularly to the Sabbath-school. It is one of your first duties in life, and an easy one. Do not let the wish to neglect it find any place in your mind."

FIRST EARNINGS.

MOST boys are inclined to be spend-thrifts. Sixpences and shillings burn holes in their pockets or slip through their fingers like so much quicksilver. It was not so with Ned Billings; though this could hardly be placed to the account of his over-carefulness of money; for money was a thing that rarely grew hot in his pockets or made his fingers uneasy. Intemperance had brought his father to an early grave; and his sad-hearted mother was laid in her last resting-place ere he was five years old. From that time he knew not the comforts of a home. An aunt gave him shelter under her roof, and a seat at her table; but both were grudgingly bestowed. As for clothing, he had little beyond what decency required. But Ned was a boy of a cheerful, buoyant temper. He went singing and laughing on his way through life, as happy, apparently, as if he were in the enjoyment of every external comfort. The common school of the village in which he lived, afforded him the rudiments of an education; and, wild and apparently reckless as he was out of school, he was rarely behind in his class. By the time he was twelve years old, Ned's mind was very well furnished for one of his age; though, to judge from his exterior, he would hardly have been thought competent to spell a word in three syllables.

The older the lad grew, the less comfortable did he find his home, and the more clearly did he perceive that his support was felt as a burden by his aunt, who hardly ever gave him a pleasant word. This was the state of affairs when, one day, as Ned was strolling idly along, a boy several years older, named Andrew Chester, the son of a storekeeper, who had been sent to carry a pretty heavy bundle to a customer who lived at some distance, called to him and said—

"I'll give you a shilling if you will take this home."

"Agreed!" was Ned's instant reply. "Where is it to go?"

"Over to Hargrove's."

Ned took hold of the bundle, and lifted it. The weight was considerable for one of his strength, and the distance to go was over a mile; but this caused no hesitation. A shilling was an amount of money so far beyond any thing he had ever possessed, that the temptation was not to be resisted.

"I'll stay here and play ball until you come back," said Andrew as he helped to place the bundle on Ned's shoulders. "I've got the shilling all ready for you." And he displayed the money before the eyes of the poor boy.

Ned started off at a quick pace; but he

had gone only a few hundred yards when he found himself staggering under a weight that was too much for his strength. Aware that if he laid it down, in order to rest, he would not be able to replace it on his shoulder again, he braced himself under his burden, and moved along as rapidly as he could walk. But, ere a third of the distance was accomplished, his strength failed, and bundle and boy both fell upon the ground. After resting for ten minutes, Ned made an effort to raise his burden; but the attempt was fruitless. A man passing at the time gave him the required assistance, and once more he started on his errand. The next resting-place for his bundle was on a fence; a hundred yards farther on, a tall stump served the same purpose. And thus, pausing to rest himself and recover his strength every twenty or thirty yards, he succeeded in accomplishing the whole distance.

When Ned came back, Andrew Chester, who had enjoyed his ball-playing for nearly an hour, paid over the shilling according to agreement. The sight of this money—a large sum in the lad's eyes—affected him with new pleasure. Here were his first earnings, and, as he looked at the coin, different thoughts from any he had heretofore known began to pass through his mind. He felt that he had in him the power to be independent. He had hands to work, feet to walk, and a willing mind.

Ned's first earnings were not spent in gratifying his appetite. He had worked too hard for his shilling to part with it lightly. Again and again he looked at the money; and each time he surveyed it, it appeared more attractive in his eyes. At last it was carefully deposited in his pocket, to be more carefully hidden away in the little garret where he slept, on his return home.

For half the night Ned lay awake, his mind too busy with the new thoughts which had entered it to sink into the oblivion of sleep. The world was opening before him, young as he was. He saw paths in which his feet could walk; and he felt eager to move in them. On the next morning, after taking a glance at his shilling, he started forth, and going to the store of Mr. Chester, saw Andrew, and asked him if he would have any more bundles for him to carry. The father of Andrew Chester, though in very good circumstances, had no idea of raising his son in idleness. He knew the value of industrious habits, and, in order to form them in Andrew, who was disposed to be indolent, he took him from school when he was fifteen, and placed him in his store. The lad was very well pleased with the change at first, for he did not much like his books. But he soon grew weary of attending in the store and carrying home goods to customers, and, whenever an opportunity offered, endeavoured to escape from the duties required of him. As his father let him have money pretty freely, he did not value it much; and had parted willingly enough with a shilling in order to escape carrying a heavy bundle for a long distance, while at the same time he secured the pleasure of an hour's sport.

The application of Ned was favourably received by Andrew; and it was agreed between them that the former should receive three cents for every package he took home for the latter, who it must be understood, did not much like to be seen carrying bundles of goods about the village. Ned, it was also agreed, should be waiting somewhere in the neighbourhood, and meet Andrew as soon as he came forth with goods in his hands. While he conveyed them to the customers, Andrew would be free to enjoy himself as he liked. For three weeks this arrangement was continued. By this time, Ned had over a dollar in his little treasury. Not a single copper had he spent in any self-indulgence. But a change came over his golden dream. Mr. Chester discovered what was going on, and, after severely reprimanding Andrew, positively forbade him making any further delegation of his work. Poor Ned was grievously disappointed when this intelligence reached his ears. Already he had begun to make calculations for the future. But the beautiful castles he had built were but airy structures, and faded away into nothingness.

The new ideas and purposes awakened in the mind of Ned could not sleep again. They were ever present before his mind. One day, a few weeks after the sudden closing of his arrangement with Andrew Chester, he said to the relative who had given him, with grudging, a home, "Aunt, if you'll give me some clothes, I'll go to New York and take care of myself."

"To York!" exclaimed the aunt, taken by surprise. "What'll you do there?"

"Work," was the confident reply. "I'm old enough and strong enough."

"You don't know what you're talking about, Ned," petulantly returned the aunt, who hardly ever gave the boy a kind word.

"Oh yes, I do," said Ned. "Only give me some decent clothes, and I'll never trouble you again as long as I live."

Ned continued to urge this point, day after day, until the aunt, becoming convinced that he was really in earnest, granted the request. A coarse suit of clothes was made up for him, and a pair of shoes and a new hat bought. With these, his dollar hid away in his pockets, as much money besides as would pay stage-hire to New York, and his aunt's blessing, such as it was, Ned turned his back upon his home and his face to the world, feeling strong and confident. A few hours' ride brought him to the great city. Never had he felt so much alone as he did while wandering along the crowded streets, which he did until the sober hues of evening reminded him that he had nowhere to lay his head. By this time he was hungry and fatigued. Not a copper had he spent since his arrival, notwithstanding the tempting array of fruit and confectionery that met his eyes at almost every turn. Now the calls of nature were not to be disregarded, and, buying some buns, he seated himself on the steps of a large house in the upper part of the city, and commenced eating his evening meal. While thus engaged, a man stopped before him, and, after looking at him for some moments, said, as if satisfied with his observation—

" Eating your supper, I see."

Ned looked an affirmative, but made no reply.

"After supper, where do you expect to sleep?" said the man, leaning as he spoke upon the iron-railing.

" I don't know," replied Ned.

" Don't know! You're from the country?"

" Yes, sir."

" What brought you to town?"

"I've come to get work and take care of myself."

"You have! When did you come?"

"To-day."

" Where from?"

"P——."

"Have you no friends in the city?"

"No, sir."

"Are your father and mother alive?"

"No, sir. I've lived with my aunt ever since I was a little boy."

"And did she let you come into the city to take care of yourself?"

"Yes, sir."

"Her affection for you must be strong," said the man, half to himself. "Have you any money?" he added.

The boy hesitated a moment or two, and then replied—

"Yes, sir."

"How much?"

"Seven shillings and sixpence."

"Where did you get this money?"

"I earned it."

"Since you came to this city?"

"No, sir: I earned it in P——. But, I couldn't get any thing more to do there, and so I thought I'd come to New York, where there was plenty of work."

Something about Ned interested the man, and as he lived in the house, he said to him, after a hurried reflection as to the propriety of doing so—

"Come in. I'd like to have some more talk with you."

Ned followed the man, who took him into his kitchen, and told a servant to give him some supper; and also to let him remain there until he sent for him.

A further interview with the lad interested the man still more. He was a lawyer, named Folwell, who had risen from a poor boy, through the force of his own character, to eminence and fortune.

"The boy needs a friend, and if he be worthy, he shall find one in me," said Mr. Folwell to himself, after his second conference with Ned. With this feeling he gave him a shelter under his roof for the night, and, on the next day, took him to his office in order to more accurately determine what was in him. To his surprise, he found that Ned could write a pretty fair hand, and could make ordinary calculations quite as well as most boys of his age. Moreover he was quick, earnest, and intelligent, and eager to enter upon any employment that was assigned him.

"He's got the right kind of stuff in him," said Mr. Folwell, after testing Ned's character and abilities in various ways. "Just such a lad as I should like to educate in my own profession."

Of course, Ned had no objection to any thing his new-found friend had to propose. It was, therefore, settled that he should enter his service and give himself up implicitly to his direction.

A year after Ned came to the city, Mr. Chester called upon Mr. Folwell, and arranged with him that his son Andrew should read law in his office. Up to this time, Ned had found but few chances of adding to his first earnings, which had never been touched beyond the sixpence it cost him for his supper on the evening of his first arrival in New York. Occasionally,

Mr. Folwell had given him a shilling to spend for himself; but the little coin had in no instance passed through his fingers, but was safely deposited to swell the treasure he was hoarding. Andrew's arrival in the city made a new era for Ned. Pocket-money had he in profusion, and, as before, he availed himself of Ned's readiness to perform almost any service, in order to gratify his natural indolence. Dollars found their way now to the boy's accumulating fund more rapidly than shillings did before.

"How much money have you, Ned?" asked Andrew, one day after he had been a year in the city.

"Six dollars," replied Ned.

"Lend it to me until week after next, and I'll pay you back seven?"

Ned hesitated.

"Don't be afraid. I'll pay it. You know I get money from home every month."

"I'm not afraid," replied Ned. "I'll

bring you the money when I come from dinner."

This was done. The six dollars were lent, and seven paid back, as agreed upon, at the time specified. Here was the beginning of new operations. Andrew now spent his money more freely, because he knew that when it was gone, he could borrow from Ned until another supply came; and the young usurer was even more eager to lend than he was to borrow. This had been going on for several months, when Mr. Folwell became aware of what was in progress. After a serious conversation with Andrew upon the folly and danger of the course of life he was adopting, he called Ned into his private office, and after referring to the subject, said to him—

"Are you not aware that what you are doing is wrong?"

"No, sir," replied Ned, looking Mr. Folwell, without a quivering eyelid, in the face.

"It is, Edward, very wrong; for you

are taking advantage of Andrew's weakness and prodigal habits, to get his money from him. I understand, that for five dollars lent to him for a week or two, he pays you six dollars. Is this so?"

"Yes, sir. He offered me that."

"But it was wrong for you to take it. You should have been willing to oblige him without the exaction of this exorbitant interest. Where did you get so much money to lend?"

"I had seven shillings and sixpence when I came here, and you have given me a good many shillings since."

"Haven't you spent any thing?"

"No, sir."

'But I haven't given you enough to make the sum of money I learn you have in possession."

"No, sir. But, since Andrew has been in New York, he has paid me a good deal for doing things for him."

"How much has he paid you for lending him money?"

"Six dollars," replied Ned, after thinking for a few moments.

"Six dollars!" Mr. Folwell shook his head and looked grave. "I don't like this at all. It's the worst thing I've seen about you, Edward."

"If I've done wrong, I'm sorry," said Ned, his face becoming serious. "I didn't know there was any harm in it."

"There is always harm in seeking our own good through injury to another," replied Mr. Folwell. "This you have done in taking the money of Andrew for a little service that you ought to have cheerfully rendered him. It put you to no inconvenience whatever in doing the favour he asked of you; but you would not grant it unless paid a most exorbitant price. Sheer selfishness, and not a spirit of good-will, influenced you. Thus your heart was hardened toward your fellows instead of being filled with kindness. This is a wrong beginning, my boy, and will lead you to grow up into a man of oppression. Why are you hoarding up your money?"

"I'm going to keep it until I become a man."

"What for?"

"I don't know."

Mr. Folwell shook his head.

"I don't like this, Edward, at all. It isn't good to love money for itself. Money is the medium of usefulness in society, and should be accumulated and used as the means of accomplishing some desired purpose. To gather and hoard it as an object of possession is wrong. No one can do it and not become a selfish, bad man. I want you to think of this. To-morrow I will talk to you again."

Ned's mind was thrown all into confusion by this unexpected reproof from Mr. Folwell. At first, he could not understand the meaning of the strange language that had been used; but, as he thought of it more and more, a dim perception of the truth began to dawn. On the next day, Mr.

Folwell again referred to the subject, and succeeded in making a stronger impression on the mind of the lad. From that time he observed him more closely, and sought in every possible way to give him higher and truer views in regard to the use of money. He induced him to spend a portion of what he had accumulated in articles that he could use in the better furnishing of his mind. For instance, he offered to pay for musical instruction, if Edward would buy himself a flute. It cost the boy a struggle to do this; but after it was done, and he commenced taking lessons, he by no means regretted the act. Thus, by ever keeping his mind on the boy's particular bias of character, Mr. Folwell was able to bend it into a better form ere it had hardened into permanency.

As for Andrew Chester, his indolence and tendency to self-indulgence were so great that little promise of future usefulness was apparent. When he was old enough to be admitted to the bar, he had nothing like the legal knowledge possessed by Edward Billings. In his first case, he paid the latter for searching out the legal authorities required for its successful presentation to the court, and gained his cause alone through the aid received from a stripling three years younger than himself. The money received for prosecuting this case constituted Andrew Chester's first earnings.

"Do you see that, Ned," said he, exhibiting a fifty-dollar bank-bill in triumph.

Edward Billings opened his eyes.

"There's my first fee! A good beginning, is it not? I'm off for Saratoga to-morrow, and don't mean to come back while a dollar of it remains."

"I wouldn't do that," said Edward.

"Why wouldn't you?" quickly asked Andrew.

"Of all money, I wouldn't waste my first earnings. Keep them as nest-eggs."

"You're a miser, Ned. A real money-lover."

"I'm not a money-waster. Dollars don't come so easily that I can afford to throw them away. But, if you will spend your first fee, do it in some useful way. Buy your mother or sister a present; or spend it in law books. Any thing but waste it in self-indulgence."

"Don't preach to me, Ned," replied Andrew, laughing. "My mother and sisters don't want any of my presents; and father has promised me a five hundred dollar library. I'm off for Saratoga; that's settled. I mean to have a good time on my first fee."

And Andrew kept his word. When he came back, every dollar of his first earnings were spent, and he applied to Edward Billings for a loan. When the latter was admitted to the bar, Andrew had obtained a very fair practice for the time he had been in the profession; but it cost him three times what he earned to live. His father, of course, made up the deficiency.

Very different from this was Edward's

manner of commencing the world. He understood too well the value of money to waste it in mere idle pleasure and personal gratification. The first fee he received was twenty dollars. Instead of spending it, as Andrew had done, he laid it carefully away to help serve as the means of his support; for, from the time of his admission to the bar, he had felt under obligation to meet entirely his own expenses. A natural feeling of independence would not permit him any longer to lean upon his kind patron. His careful habits had, during his minority, enabled him to save up about sixty dollars, which now came in as a temporary means of self-subsistence. Mr. Folwell, who had availed himself of his services for so many years, still retained them to a certain extent, and the regular amount paid to Edward for this service helped him considerably.

A few years showed the result of the different modes of entering the world pursued by the two young men. He who spent foolishly his first earnings, continued to waste what came in subsequently; and he who was careful of his first earnings continued to be careful of his after receipts.

About the time Andrew reached his twenty-seventh year, his father died; and, on the division of his property, twelve thousand dollars came to him as his share of the estate. This was in two houses in P—— and a farm in the neighbourhood. Scarcely a week elapsed after this division took place, before Andrew applied to Edward Billings for a loan of one thousand dollars on a mortgage of the farm. The latter had the money in bank, and took the mortgage. This money he had saved from his professional earnings. Andrew might have laid up money also; but as he spent his first earnings, so he continued to spend. Ten years afterward, and Edward Billings was worth twenty thousand dollars, while Andrew Chester was not worth a penny. Each had gone on as he began, and here was the result. Disheartened by this result, manner of commencing the world. He understood too well the value of money to waste it in mere idle pleasure and personal gratification. The first fee he received was twenty dollars. Instead of spending it, as Andrew had done, he laid it carefully away to help serve as the means of his support; for, from the time of his admission to the bar, he had felt under obligation to meet entirely his own expenses. A natural feeling of independence would not permit him any longer to lean upon his kind patron. His careful habits had, during his minority, enabled him to save up about sixty dollars, which now came in as a temporary means of self-subsistence. Mr. Folwell, who had availed himself of his services for so many years, still retained them to a certain extent, and the regular amount paid to Edward for this service helped him considerably.

A few years showed the result of the different modes of entering the world pursued by the two young men. He who spent foolishly his first earnings, continued to waste what came in subsequently; and he who was careful of his first earnings continued to be careful of his after receipts.

About the time Andrew reached his twenty-seventh year, his father died; and, on the division of his property, twelve thousand dollars came to him as his share of the estate. This was in two houses in P—— and a farm in the neighbourhood. Scarcely a week elapsed after this division took place, before Andrew applied to Edward Billings for a loan of one thousand dollars on a mortgage of the farm. The latter had the money in bank, and took the mortgage. This money he had saved from his professional earnings. Andrew might have laid up money also; but as he spent his first earnings, so he continued to spend. Ten years afterward, and Edward Billings was worth twenty thousand dollars, while Andrew Chester was not worth a penny. Each had gone on as he began, and here was the result. Disheartened by this result,

Chester, who had acquired dissolute habits, fell into intemperance, and gradually sank lower and lower, until he became a social cast-off—a wretched cumberer of the ground. And thus he died in the prime of manhood.

Edward Billings still lives, and is one of the most intelligent and successful members of the bar in the State of New York. He has acquired large wealth; and, he has gained it fairly. The error into which his love of accumulation first led him was properly corrected at the time when a new and healthier form was given to his growing character.

Few men succeed who do not begin right. Early errors are too frequently reproduced in all the after life. This wasting of first earnings is one of these errors. Let all who are entering the world beware how they fall into it.

SOMEBODY SEES US. Page 130.

THE LORD SEES US.

TWO little boys were walking along the road, on their way home from school, and passed by an orchard in which were trees full of ripe fruit. There was no house in sight, and no one but themselves in the road or in the fields.

"Come, Thomas," said Lewis, the elder of the two brothers, "let us go over the fence and get some nice apples. Nobody will see us?"

"I am afraid," replied Thomas.

"Why are you afraid?"

"I am sure somebody will see us."

"How can any one see us? There is

nobody in sight. Come along! I am not afraid."

After some more persuasion, Thomas said he would go, and then these two little boys climbed over the fence to take the apples that did not belong to them. That was very wrong. It was a sin against God. It was breaking one of his holy commandments. Do you know which commandment it was?—*Thou shalt not steal.* Yes, my son, that is the commandment these little boys were breaking. And they thought no one saw them. But they were mistaken.

"Who did see them?"

Listen, and you shall hear. Thomas followed his brother Lewis over the fence, and they went to a tree full of red apples, and commenced throwing up stones to knock the fruit down. Two or three beautiful apples had fallen, when Thomas, who had picked up one, and had it nearly in his pocket, let it fall, and said to his brother in a low voice, and with a look of alarm:

"Somebody does see us, Lewis."

"Who sees us?" said Lewis, dropping an apple he had just commenced eating, and looking all around.

"The Lord sees us" answered Thomas. "You know, mother says the Lord always sees us."

Lewis had two apples in his pocket, but he took them both out and threw them upon the ground, and taking his brother by the hand, said—

"Yes, the Lord sees us—I forgot that." Then the two children hurried out of the orchard as fast as they could go, and went home and told their mother what they had done, and she said to them—

"Yes, my children, the Lord always sees you: never forget that. But you should not do any thing wrong, even if the Lord could not see you. He says, *Thou shalt not steal*, and because he says so, you should never take any thing that belongs to another. It is evil to do so; and you should shun all evil as sin against God.

I am glad you have told me of your fault. Always come to me and tell me when you do wrong, and I will help you to do right."

THE PET SPARROW.

THE following pleasant story is from the French. The translation is by a friend.

Madame Helvetius, the amiable wife of the celebrated author of that name, had a remarkable fondness for birds. At her country residence a large and beautiful aviary had been fitted up, in which was a large collection of these little favourites. But this benevolent lady, aware that no luxuries can compensate for the loss of independence and liberty, allowed her guests to rove at pleasure in the neighbourhood during the day, and only closed their dwelling-place at night, to preserve them from destructive animals. It is true that, at the appearance of fine weather, the number diminished very much and few returned after the cold winds and storms of March had passed; preferring an insect picked up at random, the muddy water of a pond, the shelter of the foliage of a tree, to the grains of millet, the limpid water, and the downy nests of the aviary. In the winter, however, when it was more difficult to obtain food, numbers were again attracted to these pleasant quarters.

Madame Helvetius usually spent the winter season in Paris, whither she went toward the end of January, but she never left her then numerous and cherished guests without regret. The winter of 1788, so remarkable for its intense cold, and the great amount of suffering experienced during the first two months of the year, will long be remembered in France. The swiftest mountain streams were frozen, and some of the oldest forests partially destroyed. Beasts of prey, pressed by hunger, were to be seen prowling around the villages, plundering the sheepfolds and devouring every living thing that they could find. Travellers were frequently found upon the roads frozen to death and seemingly petrified. Thousands of birds were caught in the snares set for them, into which they rushed, enticed by the smallest morsel of food, and regardless of danger. One might almost have been led to suppose that the earth had changed its position, and that France now occupied the place of Nova Zembla or Greenland.

Madame Helvetius extended her succours to all the needy in the quarter of Paris where she was established. Her kind heart felt for all the suffering beings which surrounded her.

Her favourites, the birds, were also remembered. The windows of her apartment looked out upon a terrace, upon which she threw grain that was eagerly sought every morning by a number of sparrows which, at night, took shelter in the stables, and during the day sought everywhere for food. She delighted to step out, notwithstanding the rigour of the weather, to scatter grains to the poor birds, which would flock around, tamed by their necessities, and sometimes almost fly into her apartment.

One day, as she was standing upon the terrace, enjoying the eager haste with which the little creatures caught up the food thrown to them, a sparrow lit upon her shoulder, flew upon her hand, and then nestled in her bosom. Supposing at first that its boldness was caused by the suffering it experienced from the extreme cold, she caressed it and carried it to the fire. But perceiving that it perched familiarly on her hand, and did not appear to feel the least dread, she concluded it must be a pet of some one, which had escaped, and been attracted to the terrace, like the other birds, by the grain scattered there. After having detained the little thing for some time, Madame Helvetius, not wishing to deprive it of its liberty, opened a window, and, with a kiss, let it go, saying—

"Fly quickly, thou little wanderer, to those who doubtless regret thy loss; but if thou dost not find an asylum, return and take refuge in this bosom, which will always be ready to receive and cherish thee!"

The bird flew away, and soon disappeared among the trees of the garden.

The next day, when Madame Helvetius came out as usual upon the terrace, the same sparrow flew familiarly down upon her hand, and seemed to express by its confidence the liveliest gratitude to its kind protectress. In caressing the bird, Madame Helvetius perceived around its neck a piece of blue silk lace, to which was attached the end of the finger of a glove formed into a little bag. Passing it between her fingers, she thought she perceived the crepitation of paper; she opened it with the liveliest curiosity, and found in it a very small piece of paper folded into the narrowest compass, upon which were written several lines bearing every evidence of haste and agitation, the ink being scarcely dry. The two first lines had been changed from Racine to read—

"Thou givest food to the young of the bird,
And thy goodness extends to all nature."

Moved as much as surprised, Madame Helvetius hastened to read the rest of the billet, which contained the following:

"Virtuous persons in your vicinity are suffering from want; will you do less for them than for the numerous family which you feed every morning?"

"No!" said she, giving away to her emotion, "it would be impossible to resist a demand so touching!"

And going to the desk, she took from it a bank-note of six hundred livres, and placing it in the little bag, gave the sparrow many kisses for its commission, and let it fly. She watched carefully its flight, in the hope of discovering the house from which it had come, but it was soon lost to her view among the trees of the garden. She was at a loss to imagine how the sparrow had been taught to bear this message to her.

"By what means," said she to herself, "was it made to direct its flight toward my apartment, at the moment when I was feeding his companions in misfortune; to light upon my shoulder and to distinguish me; in a word, to choose me to relieve the sufferings of those of whom it is the charming representative? I am lost in astonishment!"

Many days passed, during which Madame Helvetius thought constantly of this singular occurrence. She mentioned it, however, to no one, as that would have been to reveal what it might be supposed she considered a meritorious action. Sometimes, too, as she had much knowledge of the world, she was inclined to believe that she might have been the dupe of some dishonest persons, for, ever, among the really the approach of spring. Madame Helvetius now vainly threw out grain upon the terrace: it attracted but a small number of her dear guests: already finding sufficient for their necessities, and already occupied in building their nests, they rarely came to this feeding-place. They appeared, indeed, to grow wilder as the fine weather approached. In the beginning of May this lady left Paris for her residence in the country, that she might repair the evils of the past winter. She hastened to restore her aviary, which had suffered some injury by the frost, to its former comfortable condition; and each time she looked upon a sparrow in her collection, her mind naturally reverted to the charming little messenger of the unknown family. Although this species of bird are not remarkable either for the variety of their songs or the beauty of their plumage, Madame Helvetius now showed a predilection for all sparrows; the reason for which was known only to her own generous heart.

Toward the middle of summer she was compelled, in consequence of some business matters, to give up her country occupations and go to Paris. A few days after her arrival, as she was inhaling the pure morning air from her pleasant terrace, she perceived the faithful sparrow, bearing upon its neck the same little bag; but it was flying about from spot to spot, seemingly undecided whether to alight, and not appearing to recognise its former friend. She vainly called it, throwing grain and making a thousand caressing signs: the bird passed and repassed, above her head, seeming to have a wish to alight, yet still fearing to do so. Madame Helvetius then thought that it might be some change of dress which caused this estrangement, and, entering her apartment, she hastily put on the winter clothing in which she had received the sparrow many months before, and reappeared upon the terrace. The bird instantaneously alighted familiarly upon her shoulder, expressing pleasure and the approach of spring. Madame Helvetius now vainly threw out grain upon the terrace: it attracted but a small number of her dear guests: already finding sufficient for their necessities, and already occupied in building their nests, they rarely came to this feeding-place. They appeared, indeed, to grow wilder as the fine weather approached. In the beginning of May this lady left Paris for her residence in the country, that she might repair the evils of the past winter. She hastened to restore her aviary, which had suffered some injury by the frost, to its former comfortable condition; and each time she looked upon a sparrow in her collection, her mind naturally reverted to the charming little messenger of the unknown family. Although this species of bird are not remarkable either for the variety of their songs or the beauty of their plumage, Madame Helvetius now showed a predilection for all sparrows; the reason for which was known only to her own generous heart.

Toward the middle of summer she was compelled, in consequence of some business matters, to give up her country occupations and go to Paris. A few days after her arrival, as she was inhaling the pure morning air from her pleasant terrace, she perceived the faithful sparrow, bearing upon its neck the same little bag; but it was flying about from spot to spot, seemingly undecided whether to alight, and not appearing to recognise its former friend. She vainly called it, throwing grain and making a thousand caressing signs: the bird passed and repassed, above her head, seeming to have a wish to alight, yet still fearing to do so. Madame Helvetius then thought that it might be some change of dress which caused this estrangement, and, entering her apartment, she hastily put on the winter clothing in which she had received the sparrow many months before, and reappeared upon the terrace. The bird instantaneously alighted familiarly upon her shoulder, expressing pleasure and

"And who is your sister, my little dear?"

"That young girl there, dressed in white, whom you see near my father and mother. The sparrow belongs to her, madame, I assure you; and she would not part with it for all the world."

She pointed out a girl of apparently sixteen or seventeen years of age, with an interesting countenance, who, blushing with joy and surprise, said to her parents—

"It is she! Yes, it is herself!"

Madame Helvetius soon found herself surrounded by the now happy family, all expressing the liveliest feelings of gratitude. The eldest daughter was so much agitated that she could not utter a word, but taking the hands of Madame Helvetius in her own, she pressed them to her heart, covering them with tears. The faithful sparrow, flying from one to another, seemed to partake of the general emotion, and completed the refreshing picture.

When, at last, the young Lise, which

was the name of the girl, found herself able to speak, she informed Madame Helvetius that she was the daughter of a carver of wood, named Valmont; that in consequence of her father's long illness and want of employment, his whole family had been reduced to the extreme of necessity. She said that the reputation of Madame Helvetius for benevolence had inspired her with the idea of trying to procure the succour for which the pride of her father would not have allowed her to make application; and that, without the knowledge of her parents, she made the attempt of sending her sparrow, the sagacity of which had enabled her to succeed beyond her most sanguine expectations.

"But I cannot understand," said Madame Helvetius, "the means by which you were enabled to direct the flight of your little messenger to my apartment."

"Oh, madame! if you knew how much pain it cost me!" replied the young Lise, caressing the sparrow, which was now nestling in her bosom. "I was compelled to expose him to the cold, and to have the cruelty to deprive him of food for entire days, that he might become attracted by the grains which you threw out to the other birds, and become familiar with you. I could see all from the window of my chamber, which looked down upon your garden. Sometimes the poor little frightened thing would, when thrust out, fly about the neighbourhood, and return after a long time, attracted by my voice; sometimes, pursued by the savage sparrows, he would return wounded by their beaks, with torn wings. At last, I saw him one day fly around you and light upon your shoulder; the next day, after having kept him from food, watching the moment when you came out upon the terrace, to scatter the grain, I ventured to send my first note. You know the rest!"

Madame Helvetius, notwithstanding the number of persons that surrounded her, was unable to restrain her emotion. She saw in this interesting occurrence, the most beautiful and touching instance of filial piety. She pressed to her heart many times the young girl, thanked her for having chosen herself as the instrument to relieve an estimable family, and begged her still to allow the dear little bird to visit her frequently.

May we not, on this occasion, say to the reader, that it is better to extend your charity to many who are unworthy, than to neglect, through fear of imposition, one who really needs assistance.

THE POWER OF KIND WORDS.

WILLIAM BAKER, and his brother Thomas and sister Ellen, were playing on the green lawn in front of their mother's door, when a lad named Henry Green came along the road, and, seeing the children enjoying themselves, opened the gate and came in. He was rather an ill-natured boy, and generally took more pleasure in teasing and annoying others than in being happy with them. When William saw him coming in through the gate, he called out to him and said, in a harsh way:

"You may just clear out, Henry Green, and go about your business! We don't want you here."

But Henry did not in the least regard what William said. He came directly forward, and joined in the sport as freely as if he had been invited instead of repulsed. In a little while he began to pull Ellen about rudely, and to push Thomas, so as nearly to throw them down upon the grass.

"Go home, Henry Green! Nobody sent for you! Nobody wants you here!" said William Baker, in quite an angry tone.

It was of no use, however. William might as well have spoken to the wind. His words were entirely unheeded by Henry, whose conduct became ruder and more offensive.

Mrs. Baker, who sat at the window, saw and heard all that was passing. As soon as she could catch the eye of her excited son, she beckoned him to come to her, which he promptly did.

"Try kind words on him," said she, "you will find them more powerful than harsh words. You spoke very harshly to

Henry when he came in, and I was sorry to hear it."

"It won't do any good, mother. He's a rude, bad boy, and I wish he would stay away. Won't you make him go home?"

"First go and speak to him in a gentler way than you did just now. Try to subdue him with kindness."

William felt that he had been wrong in letting his angry feelings express themselves in angry words. So he left his mother and went down upon the lawn, where Henry was amusing himself by trying to trip the children, with a long stick, as they ran about on the green.

"Henry," said he, cheerfully and pleasantly, "if you were fishing in the river, and I was to come and throw stones in where your line fell, and scare away all the fish, would you like it?"

"No, I should not," the lad replied.

"It wouldn't be kind in me."

"No, of course it wouldn't."

"Well, now, Henry,"—William tried to

smile and to speak very pleasantly,—" we are playing here and trying to enjoy ourselves. Is it right for you to come and interrupt us by tripping our feet, pulling us about, and pushing us down? I am sure you will not think so if you reflect a moment. So don't do it any more, Henry."

"No, I will not," replied Henry promptly. "I am sorry that I disturbed you. I didn't think what I was doing. And now I remember, father told me not to stay, and I must run home."

So Henry Green went quickly away, and the children were left to enjoy themselves.

"Didn't I tell you that kind words were more powerful than harsh words, William," said his mother, after Henry had gone away. "When we speak harshly to our fellows, we arouse their angry feelings, and then the evil spirits have power over them; but, when we speak kindly, we affect them with gentleness, and good spirits then flow into this latter state, and excite in them better thoughts and intentions. How quickly Henry changed when you changed your manner and the character of your language! Do not forget this, my son. Do not forget that kind words have double the power of harsh ones."

THE END.

www.ingramcontent.com/pod-product-compliance
Lightning Source LLC
Chambersburg PA
CBHW030313170426
43202CB00009B/986